Original title:
When Love Returns

Copyright © 2024 Swan Charm
All rights reserved.

Author: Sebastian Sarapuu
ISBN HARDBACK: 978-9916-89-877-2
ISBN PAPERBACK: 978-9916-89-878-9
ISBN EBOOK: 978-9916-89-879-6

The Ascending Heart

In prayer we find our peace,
A whisper in the dark,
Each hope a sacred ceaseless,
Our souls ignite a spark.

Among the shadows cast,
The light begins to rise,
With faith we shall hold steadfast,
And lift our eyes to skies.

The journey leads us forth,
With every step we take,
In grace we find our worth,
With love, our hearts awake.

Through valleys deep and wide,
His mercy is our guide,
In trials, we confide,
For in Him, we abide.

So let your spirit soar,
In joy, we glorify,
Together, we explore,
The realms of the Most High.

Chronicles of the Redeemed

Once lost in shadows deep,
Now found in endless light,
With every soul we keep,
In love, our hearts ignite.

The stories that we tell,
Of grace that knows no bounds,
In trials, we excel,
His voice within resounds.

From ashes, we arise,
The burdens turned to gold,
In faith, we lift our eyes,
Our spirits brave and bold.

Each moment, hear His call,
To share our light divine,
Together, we stand tall,
In truth, our lives align.

A tapestry of hope,
In fellowship, we sing,
With love, we learn to cope,
And rise on angels' wings.

The Heavenly Call of the Heart

Beneath a starry night,
A beckoning so sweet,
The heart begins its flight,
To find the pure and meet.

In silence, prayers ascend,
To realms beyond our sight,
Where every soul can mend,
And bask in holy light.

A melody of grace,
Inviting us to dwell,
In His embrace, our place,
Where love begins to swell.

The whispers of the dawn,
Guide us through every strife,
In faith, we are reborn,
Embracing eternal life.

With every beat we share,
A harmony of hope,
In unity, we dare,
And with our hearts, we cope.

Grace in the Echoing Silence

In the stillness of the night,
Whispers of love gently flow.
Grace descends, a soft, warm light,
Filling hearts with peace aglow.

In moments lost, we find our way,
Guided by a sacred hand.
Silent prayers, in shadows play,
As we learn to understand.

Each breath we take, a gift divine,
In echoes bright, our souls unite.
With every sigh, in love we shine,
In silence, we embrace the light.

The world may fade, its noise subside,
Yet in the quiet, faith is found.
With open hearts, we'll be our guide,
Within this grace, we are unbound.

Together in this sacred space,
We hold the truth, the love we seek.
In silence, we embrace His grace,
Finding strength to rise, not weak.

The Coming Home of Two Souls

When paths converge beneath the stars,
Two souls embark on journeys new.
The cosmos sings, our love's memoirs,
In sacred dance, we are renewed.

With every step, a promise made,
In whispers soft, our hearts align.
Through trials faced, no need for shade,
In love's embrace, forever shine.

Like rivers flow to endless seas,
Our spirits meet, no walls between.
In every heartbeat, hear the pleas,
Together we reclaim the dream.

The universe, a gentle guide,
In every laugh, each tear we share.
With faith as anchor, love as tide,
We find our peace in tender care.

As shadows fade, and daylight breaks,
In union strong, our spirits soar.
The home we share, no chance forsakes,
In love's embrace, forevermore.

Harmonies of the Resplendent Heart

In symphony, our spirits rise,
Melodies of love entwine.
A harmony that never dies,
Each note a gift, pure and divine.

Together we compose the song,
With every dream, a chord we find.
In sacred spaces, we belong,
With gentle grace, our hearts combined.

Through trials faced, our faith expands,
A rhythm strong, unbroken beat.
In every touch, life understands,
The dance of love, so pure and sweet.

As dawn awakens, hope renews,
In golden hues, the world's embrace.
With every breath, we chase the clues,
To find the light in love's warm grace.

In every moment, truth reveals,
The beauty in our shared delight.
Pure harmonies, our spirit heals,
Together shining, day and night.

Embracing the Divine Echo

In quiet moments, echoes call,
A presence felt, unseen but near.
With every whisper, love enthralls,
In sacred bonds, we conquer fear.

We gather strength from light above,
In unity, our hearts take flight.
Embracing endless grace and love,
We dance beneath the stars so bright.

Through valleys deep and mountains high,
The divine echoes in our souls.
With faith as wings, we learn to fly,
Together, we become our goals.

In every sunset, every dawn,
The spirit guides our wayward hearts.
With open hands, we carry on,
In love's embrace, our journey starts.

So let us rise, in hope anew,
With every step, we share the way.
Embracing echoes, strong and true,
In love's sweet song, we choose to stay.

Testament of the Heart's Revival

In shadows deep, our spirits wane,
Yet grace divine will break the chain.
With each new dawn, the heart is stirred,
Awakening hope, through love inferred.

From ashes rise the dreams once lost,
In faith we stand, whatever the cost.
The light begins to pierce the night,
Reviving us with holy light.

The whispers of the heart's true song,
Guide us where we feel we belong.
In trials faced, we find our strength,
A testament of love's great length.

With every tear, a lesson learned,
In every struggle, our souls burned.
Reconnect us, Father, in Your might,
Bring forth the day, dispel the night.

Within the silence, trust will bloom,
From barren fields to fertile room.
The heart's revival, pure and bright,
A sacred journey, bathed in light.

The Blessing of Return

Upon the path we roam so far,
Yearning hearts call from where we are.
In distant lands, we seek the truth,
Yet find our way, through humble youth.

Oh, blessed moments, lost and found,
In love's embrace, we are unbound.
Return to grace, the gentle plea,
The whispers of our destiny.

Through trials faced and burdens borne,
The heart returns, anew, reborn.
A circle formed, forever whole,
In unity, we find our soul.

With every breath, our spirits soar,
In gratitude, we seek for more.
The blessing of return is near,
A melody that we hold dear.

Embrace the dawn, the light appears,
And wash away our doubts and fears.
In sacred bond, we stand aligned,
The blessing of return, refined.

Anointed by Familiar Grace

In gentle hands, the tides shall sway,
Anointed by grace, we find the way.
Each drop of love, a sacred sign,
To heal the heart, our spirits align.

Through laughter shared and tears of pain,
In every moment, joy will reign.
The familiar grace will guide us home,
Through valleys wide, we dare to roam.

With open hearts, we'll seek and find,
The sacred truth, intertwined.
In every glance, a blessing sweet,
Familiar grace, our souls' retreat.

Let kindness flow, a river wide,
Anointed paths in love's swift tide.
Together here, we journey on,
Awash in grace, until the dawn.

So lift your voice, let praises ring,
For in our hearts, the angels sing.
Anointed by familiar grace,
In unity, we find our place.

Hymn of Reconciliation

In strife, we drift, a world apart,
Yet yearn to mend the broken heart.
With open arms, we seek to heal,
Embracing love, we dare to feel.

Oh, hymn of peace, our souls ignite,
In every shadow, find the light.
Let healing words bridge every chasm,
With gentle strength, dispel the spasm.

In humbleness, we seek to learn,
The flames of anger, let them burn.
For in forgiveness, we are free,
To build a bond, eternally.

Together now, we take a stand,
With hope and faith, we join hand in hand.
Reconciliation, sweet refrain,
Restoring joy, replacing pain.

In unity, our voices rise,
A sacred chorus fills the skies.
The hymn of love will guide our way,
In reconciliation, anew each day.

Beneath the Canopy of Grace

Beneath the canopy, we stand so still,
In whispers of faith, our hearts do fill.
The light cascades through leaves so bright,
A sacred moment, bathed in light.

With every prayer, a gentle breeze,
Brings comfort to souls, and hearts at ease.
The shadows dance in warmth and love,
A bond unbroken, sealed from above.

Each step we take in the soft earth's hue,
Is a journey embraced by grace so true.
In the quiet rustle, we're never alone,
For in His presence, we've found our home.

Divine Harmonies

In realms where angels softly sing,
The heart awakens to sacred things.
Melodies float on the breath of prayer,
A symphony woven with utmost care.

Each note a whisper, each chord a plea,
Uniting spirits in harmony free.
With hands uplifted, we join the choir,
Igniting our souls with holy fire.

In sacred stillness, the echoes remain,
Guiding us home through joy and pain.
Together we rise, in voices we soar,
With love as our anthem, forevermore.

Yielding to the Longing

In the quiet depths, a longing calls,
A voice of mercy that softly enthralls.
With open hearts, we seek the grace,
A journey of faith, a holy embrace.

As night descends, the stars ignite,
Each twinkling light, a promise of might.
We yield to love, with trust as our guide,
In the depths of darkness, we shall abide.

With every tear, the soul finds release,
In surrender, there lies sweet peace.
For in the yielding, we find our way,
To the dawn of hope, a brand new day.

A Radiant Reunion at Dusk

As dusk envelops in hues so warm,
We gather as one, safe from the storm.
With joy in our eyes, we meet again,
A radiant reunion, where love shall reign.

The sunset paints the sky with grace,
A canvas of faith, in this sacred place.
With laughter and stories, we share the night,
In fellowship's glow, everything feels right.

Hand in hand, we walk through the veil,
In shadows cast, our hearts prevail.
Embracing the moments that bring us near,
In this blessed union, we shed all fear.

The Sacred Return of Longing

In the quiet grove of prayer,
Hearts lift to the skies above.
Yearning souls find solace there,
Whispers wrapped in sacred love.

With each breath a hope reborn,
Bridging worlds both near and far.
Every tear a promise worn,
Guided by a shining star.

Through the trials, faith endures,
Seeking light in darkest night.
Longing deep fuels what is pure,
In surrender, find the right.

Gathered in the morning dew,
Voices rise like incense sweet.
In this bond, we find what's true,
Every heart, a rhythmic beat.

As we wander through the years,
With our prayers, we sow the seeds.
From the ashes, rise from fears,
In our longing, love still leads.

Emblems of Eternity

In the silence, wisdom waits,
Timeless truths stretch through the air.
Each moment holds the fates,
Threads of love in every prayer.

When the dawn breaks soft and clear,
Echoes of the ages call.
All our hopes reside right here,
Emblems of the heart enthrall.

As we gather in this space,
Stories written, souls entwined.
In each glance, a sacred grace,
In our unity, we're blind.

Like the stars that guide our way,
Shining bright in endless night.
We are but a fleeting ray,
Yet in love, we find our light.

Holding fast to faith we find,
In each heartbeat, echoes grow.
Emblems of the love, so kind,
Giving strength to all we know.

The Light of Forgiveness

In the shadows of past wrongs,
Shines a hope that calls us near.
Voices rise in sacred songs,
Forgiveness softens every fear.

Burdens lifted in the grace,
Of a heart that chooses peace.
In the warmth of love's embrace,
All our struggles find release.

Through the tears of bitter strife,
Rays of light begin to stream.
In the tapestry of life,
Forgiveness weaves a gentle dream.

Let the wounds that once held tight,
Fade beneath the brightening sky.
In each dawn, a pure delight,
From our ashes, we will fly.

Transforming hate into a gift,
With each step, the soul anew.
In forgiveness, spirits lift,
Finding strength in what is true.

Restoring an Ancient Bond

In the stillness of the night,
Whispers weave through ancient trees.
Calling forth the lost from flight,
Restoring love on gentle breeze.

Hands-in-hands, we walk the trail,
Echoes of our past align.
In the heart, where love prevails,
Bound by threads both strong and fine.

With each story told in grace,
Laughter dances, sorrow fades.
In each glance, we find our place,
In the bond that never jades.

Seek the wisdom of the wise,
In the silence, truth unfolds.
Every tear, a soft disguise,
Memory's warmth never cold.

In the embrace of night and day,
Weaving futures from the dawn.
Restoring what once slipped away,
In this love, we are reborn.

Sacred Flames Rekindled

Within the heart, a fire glows,
Divine embers, the spirit knows.
In quiet moments, grace appears,
Awakening hopes, calming fears.

The candle's flame, a guiding light,
Illuminating the darkest night.
With whispered prayers, souls entwined,
In sacred space, the truth we find.

Through trials faced, our spirits soar,
With every breath, we seek for more.
Each heartbeat sings a holy song,
In unity, we all belong.

As flames unite, we rise above,
In perfect harmony, we love.
The sacred fire, it will remain,
A symbol bright through joy and pain.

Spiritual Navigation

In the stillness of the night,
Stars align, a guiding light.
With faith's compass in our hand,
We journey forth, a promised land.

Each step we take, the path unfolds,
With ancient truths that time beholds.
The whispers of the winds we heed,
As spirits guide, in love we lead.

The currents flow, yet we stand firm,
In every trial, our hearts affirm.
With open eyes, we seek the signs,
In unity, our fate aligns.

Through valleys deep and mountains high,
We walk the earth, we touch the sky.
Together bound, we claim the grace,
In every heartbeat, our sacred space.

The Pilgrims' Sacred Bound

Upon the road, with humble feet,
We tread the path where heaven meets.
Each step a prayer, the journey long,
In every heart, a sacred song.

Through trials faced and joys embraced,
We find the spirit's warmest place.
In fellowship, we share the load,
As pilgrims walk this blessed road.

The dawn shall break, anew in grace,
With every dawn, a fresh embrace.
We travel forth, with eyes aglow,
Through love's vast realm, our spirits flow.

Each mile walked bears witness true,
To strength and hope, in all we do.
In unity, the vision clear,
The sacred bond that draws us near.

Nimbus of Reunion

In the heavens, spirits rise,
Amidst the clouds, where love belies.
A nimbus bright, with arms open wide,
Welcomes the souls from far and wide.

In every glance, a memory calls,
A tapestry woven, as the heart enthralls.
Through time and space, we intertwine,
In every beat, our souls align.

Amidst the storms and skies of gray,
The light within shall guide the way.
Together bound in sacred grace,
In unity, we find our place.

The reunion sweet, our spirits sing,
With every breath, new hopes take wing.
In the nimbus bright, love's embrace,
We find our peace, our sacred space.

Symphony of the Longing Heart

In silence whispers the yearning soul,
A melody of faith begins to rise.
Each note a prayer, a distant goal,
With every heartbeat, the spirit flies.

From shadows deep, the light breaks through,
Guiding the heart on a sacred quest.
In love's embrace, we find what's true,
The longing heart seeks eternal rest.

A symphony played on strings of grace,
Echoes of love in the eternal night.
Each harmony a touch, a sacred space,
Where the heart finds solace, pure and bright.

Embraced by the stars, the moonlight glows,
The journey long, yet divine in its art.
In every trial, the spirit grows,
The symphony sings of a longing heart.

The Holy Pilgrims of Affection

With every step, the pilgrims tread,
In faith they walk, hand in hand.
On pathways paved with words unsaid,
They seek the love of the promised land.

Through valleys low and mountains high,
They carry hope, a lantern bright.
In unity, their spirits fly,
Guided by faith, they brave the night.

With fervent hearts, they sing their song,
Of love that binds, transcending time.
In every note, where they belong,
Their lives a prayer, a soaring rhyme.

The holy light is all around,
In the shared moments, a sacred bond.
In every heartbeat, a love unbound,
The pilgrims stand steadfast and fond.

Tapestry of Devotion

In threads of gold and beams of light,
A tapestry of love unfolds.
Each woven heart, a sacred sight,
In devotion, the story holds.

With every stitch, a promise made,
To honor the journey, a bond so deep.
In every color, joy and shade,
The tapestry speaks while the world sleeps.

In moments shared, the fibers dance,
With laughter and tears, both rich and rare.
Together they weave a holy trance,
Each strand a testimony of care.

As the loom spins fast, the spirit sings,
Of hearts entwined, of love's embrace.
In the fabric of life, we find our wings,
A tapestry woven of endless grace.

A Celestial Ballet

In twilight's glow, the stars do twirl,
A celestial ballet in the night sky.
Each movement whispers, hearts unfurl,
In the dance of love, the spirits fly.

The moonlight casts a silver beam,
On galaxies spinning, a sacred art.
In every step, a sacred dream,
The cosmos echoes the beat of the heart.

As comets streak with fiery trails,
The dancers leap in joyous flight.
In harmony, the universe exhales,
The ballet of souls, alive and bright.

In love's embrace, the stardust sways,
In perfect rhythm, a divine connection.
Forever spinning, through all our days,
In this celestial ballet, we find affection.

Finding Eden Once More

In whispered prayers we seek the sun,
Where verdant pastures breathe as one.
The gates of grace swing wide with ease,
As spirits rise on gentle breeze.

In every heart a garden grows,
With seeds of love that heaven sows.
Each blossom tells of sacred truth,
In innocence, the glow of youth.

The rivers flow with life anew,
A promise held, a bond so true.
In harmony, the angels sing,
As joy and peace to souls we bring.

The light that breaks the shadows vast,
Reveals the future, frees the past.
With faith, we walk on pathways bright,
In Eden's arms, our souls take flight.

As we return to what we lost,
Embrace the journey, count the cost.
For every step, a stone of grace,
In finding Eden, we find our place.

Illuminated by Your Presence

In stillness of the evening prayer,
We breathe the love that fills the air.
Your light, a beacon in the night,
Illuminates our path so bright.

With every heartbeat, echoes sound,
In sacred whispers, we are found.
A symphony of grace and peace,
In You, our worries find release.

The stars above, they dance and sing,
In every moment, hope takes wing.
Your faithfulness, a guiding hand,
In darkness, Lord, we understand.

With thankful hearts, we lift our praise,
In quiet awe, our spirits gaze.
Through trials faced and storms we ride,
In Your embrace, we will abide.

For every shadow must give way,
To morning's light, to dawning day.
In Your presence, fears are torn,
And in Your love, our hearts reborn.

The Divine Return of Promise

In the quiet dawn, the promise stirs,
A gift divine, in hearts of hers.
With every moment, hope remains,
A testament through joys and pains.

The heavens shout, their chorus bold,
In stories of the faith retold.
When tears are shed, and spirits tire,
Your presence brings the heart's desire.

Through barren lands, Your light will shine,
A path restored, a love divine.
In trials met, we find our song,
To You alone, we all belong.

As seasons change, and rivers flow,
In every heart, Your seeds we sow.
With arms outstretched, we seek the grace,
To find the strength in Your embrace.

The promise whispered in the night,
A steady flame, our guiding light.
With every breath, we choose to stand,
The Divine return, Your perfect plan.

Reflections from the Ruins

Amid the stones where shadows play,
Past echoes linger, hopes decay.
Yet in the dust, a spark will gleam,
A fractured world, still holds a dream.

The ruins speak of battles fought,
In every scar, a lesson taught.
With love and faith, we hold to light,
In darkest days, we find our fight.

From crumbled heights, our vision grows,
A phoenix born from ashes' rose.
In every heart where sorrow dwells,
The sweetest hymn of hope compels.

With every prayer, we rebuild trust,
In sacred vows, we rise from dust.
Together strong, we weave anew,
A tapestry of love so true.

For in these ruins, grace abounds,
In whispered dreams, life's purpose sounds.
And from the depths, we take our stand,
Through reflections clear, we heed Your hand.

Seraphic Yearning

In the stillness of the night,
Hearts are lifted, pure in sight.
Whispers of grace, softly sway,
Guiding souls to find their way.

With faith as bright as morning dew,
A longing deep, so fierce and true.
Voices raised in sacred song,
To the heavens, where we belong.

Angels dance in the light divine,
A touch of God, a love enshrined.
Each prayer sent, like incense rise,
Filling space through open skies.

Yearning hearts in unity plea,
For peace on earth, for all to see.
In silence pure, where dreams ignite,
Those seraphic visions take flight.

Embrace the hope in every breath,
A promise born, overcoming death.
With spirits joined, we seek the flame,
Of longing hearts that call His name.

The Altar of Togetherness

Upon the altar, hands entwined,
We gather here, in Spirit aligned.
Hearts ablaze with love profound,
In sacred bonds, our souls unbound.

Each word a prayer, a whispered vow,
In unity, we humbly bow.
The warmth of fellowship we share,
An answered call, a sacred prayer.

Sunrise breaks, a brand new day,
Together strong, come what may.
We lift our voices, strong and bright,
In the glow of God's pure light.

As one, we stand, no fear remains,
In joy and sorrow, love sustains.
A tapestry of hope we weave,
In every heart, we come to believe.

Through trials faced in love's embrace,
We find our strength, our hallowed space.
In faith we forge, a truth so clear,
The altar of togetherness draws near.

Wings of Redemption

Beneath the weight of heavy chains,
We long for light, for love that reigns.
With open hearts, we seek the way,
To find the grace in each new day.

The lost and weary find a guide,
In arms of mercy, we confide.
With wings of hope, our spirits soar,
To heights unknown, forevermore.

Forgiven pasts, we lay to rest,
In every soul, His love, our quest.
A journey vast, with faith our steed,
On wings of redemption, we are freed.

In shadows cast, His light will shine,
Transforming hearts, a love divine.
Rebirth bestowed in gentle breath,
In unity, we conquer death.

By grace we rise, anew we stand,
In sacred bonds, together hand in hand.
Our spirits woven, free to dance,
In wondrous love, we take our chance.

A Covenant Restored

In twilight's glow, a promise made,
Through stormy nights, our fears allayed.
With every heartbeat, trust resounds,
A covenant restored, love abounds.

The sacred ties, once torn apart,
Now stitch together every heart.
With whispered dreams of dawn's embrace,
We gather near, to seek His grace.

In patience taught, we learn to wait,
For love's sweet song, it conquers fate.
A bond renewed by faith's decree,
United souls, forever free.

In sacred rituals, we draw near,
With every tear, we shed our fear.
Through trials faced, His light we find,
A perfect love, in peace aligned.

With open arms, He calls us home,
Through every path, no more we roam.
A covenant sealed, in love we trust,
In God's embrace, we rise, we must.

Rekindled Devotion

In the silence of prayer, I kneel,
Whispers of love, the soul can feel.
Heaven's light shines upon my face,
In the arms of grace, I find my place.

With every dawn, my heart awakes,
Faithful vows, the spirit makes.
A spark ignites, divine embrace,
In the warmth of love, I find my trace.

Through trials faced, my faith did grow,
In darkest nights, Your light would show.
I surrender all, to sacred trust,
In Your mercy, Lord, I rise from dust.

As rivers flow to oceans vast,
In Your love, my heart is cast.
With every heartbeat, a sacred song,
In devotion rekindled, I belong.

Each moment cherished, my soul renewed,
In passion's fire, my spirit brewed.
With every thought of You, I thrive,
In rekindled devotion, I am alive.

Epiphany of the Heart's Desire

In quiet moments, truth revealed,
A gentle touch, my heart is healed.
Desires whispered in the night,
In love's embrace, we find the light.

Awakening dreams, a sacred dance,
Guided by fate, a timeless chance.
In the stillness, I hear Your call,
My heart rejoices, I surrender all.

Through storms and trials, I have roamed,
Yet in Your presence, I feel at home.
A luminous path, my spirit soars,
In epiphany found, love opens doors.

With every prayer, a longing deep,
In trust and faith, my soul does leap.
Heart's desire, pure and true,
In sacred union, I am renewed.

The journey unfolds with every breath,
In love's embrace, there is no death.
Epiphany shines, guiding me near,
In heart's desire, I hold You dear.

Navigating to the Source

With compass set, my heart takes flight,
In search of grace, I seek the light.
Through mountains high and valleys low,
Navigating paths where faith must grow.

Each step unfolds a sacred quest,
In trials faced, I find my rest.
The Source of all, my guiding star,
In every struggle, You are never far.

Waves of doubt crash against my shore,
Yet in Your strength, I rise once more.
A beacon shines through every storm,
In Your embrace, I am reborn.

The river flows, pure and divine,
In currents strong, my spirit aligns.
With every turn, I seek and strive,
To find the Source where dreams revive.

Through prayer and hope, my path is clear,
With faith as anchor, I persevere.
Navigating toward the Sacred Light,
In the Source of love, my heart takes flight.

A Chorus of Second Chances

In the silence, echoes rise,
A chorus sings beneath the skies.
Each note a promise, sweet and true,
In second chances, I'm born anew.

When shadows fall, and doubts invade,
Your love shines bright, a serenade.
With open arms, You call my name,
In the dance of grace, I'm free from shame.

Through broken paths, my spirit roams,
Yet in Your heart, I find my home.
A melody of hope, softly played,
In every moment, I'm unafraid.

Each stumble met with tender grace,
In second chances, I find my place.
With every tear, a lesson learned,
In the sacred fire, my soul is burned.

Together we rise, hand in hand,
In the beauty of life, we understand.
A chorus flows, of love's embrace,
In second chances, we find our space.

The Sacred Reunion

Beneath the stars that guide our way,
We gather in the light of day.
Hearts entwined, we seek the call,
In love's embrace, we stand tall.

Voices whisper in the breeze,
A testament to faith's sweet ease.
In every tear, a joy reborn,
From sorrow's dusk, our spirits worn.

Together we tread the sacred ground,
In unity, our souls are bound.
With every step, we find our place,
In the warmth of Divine grace.

Hands uplifted, we share our dreams,
In heartfelt songs, our hope redeems.
Through shadows deep, we seek the light,
A sacred reunion, our souls ignite.

In every laugh, in every prayer,
The power of love fills the air.
With voices lifting, spirits soar,
In our reunion, we seek no more.

Echoes of the Heart's Pilgrimage

Across the valleys where silence dwells,
The heart's pilgrimage, a tale it tells.
Through trials faced and mountains high,
In faith we journey, never shy.

Each step a rhythm, each breath a prayer,
In the echoing beauty, we find repair.
A sacred map, drawn in love,
Guided gently by forces above.

In the scattered leaves of autumn's breath,
We ponder life, we ponder death.
And in the twilight, what wisdom awaits,
The heart rejoices, love never waits.

With every whisper of the gentle night,
The stars remind us of our sacred light.
Each echo reverberates the truth,
That love transcends the bounds of youth.

In fields of grace, we plant our seeds,
The heart's pilgrimage fulfills our needs.
In echoes soft, we find the way,
To rise anew, to greet the day.

Embrace of the Wanderer's Soul

Amidst the paths both wide and narrow,
The wanderer's heart seeks love to borrow.
In sights unseen and dreams unknown,
He finds the seeds of truth are sown.

With silent prayers upon the breeze,
The wanderer's soul finds sweet release.
In every corner of the earth,
A tapestry of life and rebirth.

Through winding roads and endless skies,
The embrace of love ignites the wise.
Each moment cherished, a fleeting glance,
The wanderer dances in life's vast expanse.

In every star that lights the night,
A reminder of love's endless flight.
With faith as compass, hope the goal,
The sacred journey, the wanderer's soul.

Through trials faced and victories won,
The wanderer's heart has just begun.
In every setback, the seeds of grace,
An embrace of the Divine we trace.

Divine Serendipity

In moments fleeting, grace does flow,
A dance of fate, a gentle glow.
In serendipity, we find the light,
Divine impressions, day and night.

Wandering softly through life's embrace,
We catch a glimpse of sacred space.
Each smile exchanged, a blessing shared,
In this grand journey, we are prepared.

As rivers merge and oceans blend,
Life's divine path knows no end.
In the laughter spilled beneath the sun,
Serendipity reveals we are one.

In trials transformed, we find our way,
Through swirling storms, we learn to stay.
With every heartbeat, love's melody,
We dance in rhythm with divinity.

In the quiet moments, still and pure,
Divine serendipity opens the door.
With hearts aligned, we walk this path,
In grace's presence, we find our laugh.

Anointed in Tenderness

In whispers soft, the heart is blessed,
With gentle hands, the soul finds rest.
A light descends, pure love bestowed,
In sacred silence, grace is flowed.

The weary find their strength anew,
In tender moments, spirits grew.
Each tear transforms into a prayer,
For in the sorrow, kindness rare.

Embrace the warmth of love divine,
Through humble paths, His light will shine.
In every heartbeat, hope is sown,
Anointed in tenderness, not alone.

As dawn breaks forth with vibrant hue,
Our praises rise, a joyful view.
In touch of faith, we stand as one,
With open hearts, our race is run.

In every trial, His voice we hear,
With faith like rivers, we persevere.
Through kindness shown, His love transcends,
Anointed forever, our journey bends.

The Swell of Sacred Resurgence

From depths of darkness, light does rise,
A swell of hope, the heart complies.
In stillness, whispers of rebirth,
A holy promise, sacred worth.

The waves of faith shall cleanse our pain,
Each struggle faced shall not be vain.
In trials met, our spirits soar,
With every heartbeat, we restore.

The sun shall rise on weary days,
In golden hues, our spirit plays.
With hands uplifted, we will sing,
For in His grace, our souls take wing.

The earth will tremble with new life,
As love abounds, dispelling strife.
In every dawn, a gift we see,
A swell of sacred unity.

Rejoice in strength through every storm,
In love's embrace, our hearts are warm.
A sacred journey, we engage,
With faith as our eternal gauge.

The Embrace of Reunion

Lost in the shadows, we seek the light,
Through every silence, love ignites.
In arms wide open, forgiveness found,
The embrace of reunion, glory unbound.

With every step, a circle closed,
In shared embrace, our hearts exposed.
The sacred bond that time can't sever,
In gentle whispers, we are tethered.

From ashes rise, new life takes form,
With love's embrace, we weather the storm.
The broken pieces, all made whole,
In reunion's warmth, we find our role.

In every journey marked by grace,
We share the love in every space.
Hand in hand, we face the day,
In unity's glow, we choose to stay.

Through eyes of mercy, we perceive,
In every moment, we believe.
The embrace of reunion shines so bright,
In love eternal, we find our light.

A Parable of Joy

In fields adorned with endless bloom,
A tale of joy dispels all gloom.
With humble hearts, we gather round,
In laughter's echo, peace is found.

A coin of kindness, freely shared,
In simple acts, our souls are bared.
From small beginnings, joy will grow,
A parable, in love we sow.

The sun will rise on every smile,
In gentle hearts, we'll walk a mile.
With voices raised, our songs will soar,
In joy, we find forevermore.

The wonders of the world unfold,
In every story, truths are told.
A dance of faith, so full of grace,
In joy's embrace, we find our place.

So let us cherish every day,
In love and laughter, come what may.
For in each moment, life's sweet spark,
A parable of joy ignites the dark.

Glory in the Embrace of Forgiveness

In shadows deep, grace shines bright,
A heart once heavy, now takes flight.
With every tear, a lesson learned,
In love's embrace, our spirits turned.

From trials faced, we rise anew,
In mercy's light, we find what's true.
Forgive us, Lord, as we forgive,
In Your embrace, we truly live.

The burden lifted, chains set free,
In unity, we bend the knee.
The past dissolves, a sacred space,
In glory found, we seek Your grace.

With open hearts, we sing Your praise,
In every moment, feel Your gaze.
For in forgiveness, we find peace,
In love's embrace, our souls release.

Rejoicing in the light of day,
We walk the path, in faith we stay.
In glory's name, our spirits soar,
In You, O Lord, forevermore.

Resurgence in Sacred Harmony

Beneath the stars, where silence speaks,
A melody of hope it seeks.
In sacred rhythm, life unfolds,
With every note, our hearts behold.

The whispers of the heart emerge,
In harmony, our spirits surge.
With faith as guide, we start anew,
In sacred songs, we worship You.

When shadows fall and doubts arise,
We lift our voices to the skies.
The joy of love, a guiding flame,
In every song, we breathe Your name.

Connected in this cosmic dance,
In sacred space, we find our chance.
In every breath, Your essence flows,
In resonance, our spirit grows.

Together, we shall rise above,
In unity, we find Your love.
A resurgence bold, in harmony,
In reverence, Lord, we long to be.

The Pilgrimage Back to You

Through winding paths, our feet shall tread,
In search of light, where hope is fed.
With every step, our hearts we raise,
In quest of truth, we give You praise.

The mountains high, the valleys wide,
In every trial, You are our guide.
With steadfast hearts, we journey on,
To You, O Lord, we sing our song.

In every shadow, love's embrace,
Through tears and joy, we seek Your face.
The pilgrimage of faith we roam,
In every heart, we find our home.

With open hands, we seek Your will,
In quiet moments, our hearts be still.
The road may twist, but still we find,
In sacred truth, our souls entwined.

As dawn breaks forth and shadows flee,
In unity, we find the key.
The pilgrimage leads us to You,
In every heart, Your love is true.

An Offering of Love's Return

In humble prayer, we lift our hands,
An offering of love that understands.
With grateful hearts, we seek to share,
The blessings found in Your sweet care.

Through trails of doubt, we walk in trust,
In every act, a love combusts.
With open eyes, we see the light,
In unity, we find our might.

Each moment spent in gratitude,
Transforms our hearts from solitude.
In loving kindness, we shall grow,
An offering pure, our spirits glow.

In giving back, we find our gain,
In every joy, we share the pain.
Together bound, our spirits yearn,
In love's sweet dance, we softly turn.

The world around may fade to gray,
Yet in Your light, we find our way.
An offering dear, we now return,
In love's embrace, our souls discern.

Pathways to the Beloved

In the quiet dawn, we seek the light,
A guiding star, shining ever bright.
With every step on sacred ground,
In whispered prayers, true peace is found.

Through valleys low, and mountains high,
Hearts draw near, as spirits fly.
In unity, the lost shall roam,
Each path leads back to love's sweet home.

Beneath the sky, a tapestry woven,
Threads of faith, eternally chosen.
The paths converge, with hope we tread,
In sacred circles, where souls are fed.

Awake my heart, to love's embrace,
In every heartbeat, find your grace.
For on this journey, side by side,
Together we walk, forever allied.

Blessed Whispers of Reconnection

In the silence, a voice calls near,
Whispers of love, for those who hear.
Bridges built with gestures small,
In gentle words, we rise, we fall.

Softly spoken in sacred rhyme,
Each note a thread of love divine.
In every rhythm, pulses align,
Bringing forth strength, in hearts that shine.

Across the ages, a bond renewed,
In shared moments, our spirits moved.
With open arms, we gather here,
In blessed whispers, we shed all fear.

Let the past dissolve, be swept away,
Hold the light of a brand new day.
In the stillness, find our way home,
Boundless journeys, we will roam.

Sundering the Veil of Time

Through the mists of time, we wander free,
Eternal souls in unity.
The veil parts softly, revealing truth,
In every heartbeat, lies the proof.

Moments cherished, yet time unfolds,
In stories whispered, wisdom bold.
As rivers flow and seasons change,
We find the threads of love arrange.

Cast aside the weight of years,
In sacred hope, dissolve your fears.
For in this space, the past and now,
Merge together, a sacred vow.

As dawn breaks through the darkest night,
The sun shall rise, in glorious light.
In timeless embrace, find solace true,
For love endures, in all we do.

The Graceful Return of Familiar Echoes

In echoes soft, our voices blend,
A symphony of hearts, without end.
The songs of old, now weave anew,
In every note, a love so true.

Through laughter shared and tears that flow,
In every moment, our spirits glow.
Resonate with each profound sigh,
In gentle breaths, our souls reply.

The circle turns, as time reveals,
In every hardship, our fate heals.
With graceful steps, we dance as one,
In sacred rhythms, our souls have spun.

Return we must to love's embrace,
In every heart, we find our place.
As echoes linger, forever near,
In love's great tapestry, we persevere.

In the Temple of Rediscovery

In shadows deep, we search for light,
A sacred space, where souls take flight.
Amid the whispers, grace unfolds,
Revealing truths that time upholds.

With open hearts, we gather near,
A chorus rises, soft but clear.
In every prayer, a healing balm,
Restoring peace, embracing calm.

The walls of stone, now warm and bright,
Embody love, dispelling fright.
We tread the path of ancient rites,
Reclaiming joy on sacred nights.

In every tear, a lesson found,
In every laugh, a holy sound.
Together, hand in hand we stand,
Awakening the spirit's land.

And as we leave, we carry grace,
A gentle touch, a warm embrace.
In the temple of rediscovery,
We find our way, we find our plea.

A Chorus of Hope's Return

Through valleys dark, a light breaks forth,
A chorus sings of joy and worth.
Each note a promise, whispered sweet,
Guiding the weary, lifting feet.

In troubled times, we find our guide,
With faith as anchor, love our stride.
United voices, strong and bold,
We weave a tapestry of gold.

The winds may shift, but still we hold
To dreams of peace, to visions told.
Through trials fierce, we learn to soar,
With wings of hope, we seek for more.

A glimmer shines in every heart,
A spark of light, a brand new start.
Together strong, we face the morn,
A chorus sweet, in faith reborn.

And as we walk this rugged way,
We raise our song, come what may.
For in the echo of our yearn,
Is found the hope of love's return.

The Reclamation of Tender Vows

In twilight's grasp, where promises lie,
We gather close, beneath the sky.
With gentle hands, we weave anew,
The threads of love, forever true.

In whispered words, our hearts reflect,
The vows we've made, our lives connect.
Through testing storms, we stand as one,
In sacred trust, our journey's begun.

The past may haunt, but not define,
For in this moment, our lives align.
Each tear a drop, each smile a rose,
In affection's dance, our spirit grows.

With every beat, our rhythms blend,
In faithful hearts, we find our mend.
Together facing what's to come,
In love's embrace, we find our home.

And as the stars take radiant flight,
We hold each other through the night.
The reclamation of tender vows,
In love's sweet grace, we find our brows.

The Gift of Faithful Return

In every season, hearts may stray,
But faith still calls, it lights the way.
A journey long, with lessons steep,
In every sorrow, treasures keep.

With every sunset, shadows fade,
A promise made, our fears allayed.
In gentle breezes, whispers tell,
Of love that holds, of hope that swells.

In quiet moments, we reflect,
A tapestry of life we knit.
With wisdom gained from trials faced,
In faithful return, our souls embraced.

Through storms we've weathered, hand in hand,
Together strong, we make our stand.
In laughter shared, in tears we yearn,
The gift of faithful hearts, we learn.

And when the dawn breaks, new and bright,
We rise again, united light.
For in the journey of our days,
The gift of love forever stays.

Sacred Whispers of the Soul

In the stillness of the night,
Voices echo softly near,
Guiding hearts towards the light,
Where love dissolves all fear.

Angels sing in gentle tones,
Woven in the fabric bright,
Every prayer a sacred stone,
Casting shadows into light.

Breathe the air of holy grace,
Feel the warmth of endless care,
In this hallowed, sacred space,
Hope and peace entwine the air.

Eternal love shines radiant,
Through the trials we embrace,
In each moment, variant,
We find refuge in His grace.

So let whispers guide our way,
On this journey of the soul,
Trust in what the heart will say,
For His love will make us whole.

A Love Resurrected

From the depths of darkest night,
A love arose, pure and strong,
In the dawn, a guiding light,
Binding hearts where they belong.

Through the valleys of despair,
Hope ignited a bright flame,
Whispers carried on the air,
In His love, we found our name.

Every tear a lesson learned,
In the fires of sacred grace,
From the ashes, hearts returned,
Finding strength in love's embrace.

Stars align in perfect dance,
Each heartbeat, blessed and true,
In this life, a second chance,
Love revived, forever new.

Let us rise, our spirits soar,
Hand in hand, we walk the way,
In love's arms, forevermore,
Guided by the light of day.

The Pilgrimage of Affection

On the winding road we tread,
Each step echoes love's sweet song,
In the heart, no fear or dread,
Together, where we belong.

With every stone, a tale unfolds,
Of the journey, rich and deep,
In the warmth of hands we hold,
Promises our souls will keep.

Mountains rise, and rivers flow,
Tests of faith we gladly face,
In the light of love, we grow,
Finding joy in every trace.

As the sun paints skies with gold,
We march on in sacred trust,
In this love, our dreams unfold,
Bound by hearts and endless gust.

Together on this path we walk,
Every turn a story told,
Faith and love in perfect talk,
In affection, we are bold.

Chosen Paths in Light

In the stillness, we are called,
To the paths where light abides,
Every shadow gently stalled,
In His grace, our heart confides.

With each breath, the spirit grows,
Guiding us through trials faced,
In the bloom of love that flows,
Find the beauty, deeply placed.

Steps of faith we take with ease,
Trusting in the love bestowed,
In His presence, hearts find peace,
Walking on the chosen road.

In the tapestry of life,
Threads of joy and sorrow weave,
Through the silence and the strife,
In His light, we all believe.

Let us share this sacred dance,
Through each moment, pure and bright,
In our hearts, the same romance,
Chosen paths forever light.

Journey to the Heart's Conclave

Through valleys deep where shadows play,
We seek the light of dawning day.
With hearts aligned, we walk the path,
To find the peace within the wrath.

Each step a prayer, each breath a hymn,
In whispered love, we seek to swim.
The sacred silence calls us near,
In every pulse, the truth appears.

Beneath the stars, in night's embrace,
We feel the warmth of spirit's grace.
The journey leads to sacred ground,
Where holy voices can be found.

The river flows with wisdom pure,
In nature's grasp, we feel secure.
In every tear, the joy is sown,
The heart's conclave is love's own throne.

So we shall walk, undaunted still,
With faith anew, our hearts fulfill.
Together bound in love's decree,
The journey leads us back to Thee.

The Sacred Cycle of Comeback

In every loss, a seed is sown,
To break the soil, to make us grown.
The sun will rise, the moon will wane,
In every joy, we glean the pain.

Life's rhythm dances, ebb and flow,
In every tear, a chance to grow.
The wheel of time spins round and round,
A sacred cycle, grace is found.

Through trials faced, we find our way,
To brighter shores, to light of day.
With every heartbeat, we are blessed,
In hope renewed, our souls find rest.

The storm will pass, the skies will clear,
With faith in heart, we lose our fear.
The sacred bond of life remains,
In every loss, a love regains.

So rise again, embrace the strife,
For in the struggle lies our life.
A comeback forged in love's own flame,
Forever changed, we're never same.

Illumination in Shared Dreams

In twilight's glow, we find our way,
Through whispers soft, the night holds sway.
With open hearts, we dare to see,
The dreams that blend in harmony.

Each vision shared, a sacred thread,
In woven stories, hope is fed.
Together we rise, together we fall,
In shared embrace, we hear love's call.

The tapestry of dreams unfurls,
In each encounter, magic swirls.
With every gaze, the stars ignite,
Illumination shines so bright.

As souls connect in pure delight,
The night reveals its deepest light.
In sacred space, we bloom and grow,
In love's embrace, we come to know.

So let us dream, together soar,
In every heartbeat, linger more.
In shared dreams, we heal and mend,
The light of love shall never end.

The Beloved's Midnight Prayer

In quiet hours, the world stands still,
The heart attunes to deepened will.
A prayer ascends on gentle sighs,
In midnight's hush, our spirits rise.

With faith as warmth, our souls unite,
In sacred whispers, find the light.
The Beloved hears our humble plea,
In every breath, we long to see.

Through darkest nights, we seek the way,
In love's sweet presence, fears allay.
Each word a thread in heaven's loom,
A tapestry of grace in bloom.

In solitude, the heart finds voice,
With every tear, we make the choice.
To trust in love, to carry on,
In every dusk, behold the dawn.

So lift the heart, embrace the night,
For in the shadows, shines the light.
The Beloved's prayer, our souls entwined,
In midnight's grace, our hearts aligned.

The Light That Unites

In silence whispers truth of grace,
The light that binds each soul in place.
With faith, we rise, hand in hand,
Our spirits soar, a faithful band.

Each moment shared, a sacred thread,
In love's embrace, we gently tread.
Through trials faced, we find our way,
United in the dawn of day.

The sacred flame within us glows,
Illuminating paths we chose.
With every heartbeat, every prayer,
The light shines bright, our burdens bare.

The bond of hearts, a pact divine,
In quiet hours, the stars align.
Together we ascend the heights,
In harmony, we share our lights.

In faith's embrace, our souls take flight,
One chorus sings, from dark to light.
The truth of love will guide us home,
In unity, we are never alone.

Journey Towards the Divine

Upon this path, we seek the grace,
A journey vast, in every place.
With hearts aglow, we move ahead,
In sacred steps, by faith we're led.

Moments gleam with wisdom's light,
Through shadows cast, we find our sight.
Each tear a seed, each smile a gain,
Through joy and grief, in love we reign.

The mountain high, the valley low,
In every challenge, strength will grow.
With spirits bold, we journey forth,
To touch the heavens, seek the worth.

A tapestry of souls entwined,
In prayerful whispers, hearts aligned.
Together we ascend the skies,
In unity, our spirits rise.

In every prayer, we lift the veil,
Of earthly ties; love will prevail.
Towards the divine, we walk with grace,
In every step, we find our place.

Shattering the Veil of Distance

A heart can bridge the widest sea,
In love, we find our destiny.
With every thought, the distance fades,
In sacred bonds, the truth cascades.

Through trials faced, we stand as one,
As morning rises with the sun.
Beyond the gaze of worldly strife,
In unity, we find our life.

The veil of distance, but a guise,
In every prayer, true love will rise.
With every pulse, across the miles,
Connection thrives, and hope beguiles.

In echoes soft, our spirits dance,
A sacred bond, a timeless chance.
In every moment, every breath,
We conquer fear, defy the death.

With hearts entwined, we reach above,
Creating worlds with acts of love.
In faith's embrace, we break the night,
Together shining, ever bright.

When Time Folds Back

In quiet moments, time will bend,
To spaces where beginnings blend.
With every heartbeat, echoes call,
Reminding us, we are not small.

In silence, wisdom breaks the chain,
Where past and future meet again.
With open hearts, we find our way,
In every dusk, there blooms a day.

The lessons learned, the paths we trace,
In every choice, we find our place.
With eyes that see beyond the veil,
Our journeys weave a sacred tale.

For time is but a flowing stream,
In faith, we hold to every dream.
As moments shift, we find our soul,
In unity, we're truly whole.

In love's embrace, the past ignites,
With every tear, the future writes.
When time folds back, we stand in grace,
Infinite light in every space.

A Sacred Song of Reunion

In whispers soft, the spirits call,
As hearts unite beneath the thrall.
In sacred spaces, love takes flight,
A melody that graces night.

With every tear, the past must yield,
In faith and hope, the wounds are healed.
Together we rise, hand in hand,
Bound by a light only love can command.

Through trials faced, we shall not part,
For every beat, you own my heart.
In laughter's echo, pure and sweet,
We find our joy, our souls complete.

The journey long, yet we are one,
In every deed, our love is spun.
With grace surrounding, we ascend,
In this communion, no bitter end.

Awake, dear soul, for dawn is near,
In sacred song, we draw you here.
Together we'll dance 'neath stars so bright,
In love's embrace, we face the night.

The Ascendancy of Commitment

In steadfast vows, our spirits soar,
Together in faith, we seek to explore.
With every promise, we plant a seed,
In love's rich soil, we'll find our creed.

Through storms that rage and trials long,
In unity's bond, we grow strong.
Our hearts aligned in purpose clear,
With grace as our guide, we hold dear.

In moments quiet, we find our strength,
With open arms, we embrace the length.
Through every shadow, we will tread,
For commitment's light shall guide us ahead.

With every breath, we pledge again,
In sacred spaces, there is no end.
For love's ascent, as yours and mine,
In devotion pure, our lives entwine.

Beyond the trials, joy awaits,
In commitment's arms, we elevate.
With hearts alight, and spirits free,
Together we forge eternity.

Elysium in Each Other's Eyes

In your gaze, the heavens gleam,
A world alive, a timeless dream.
With every look, the softest sigh,
In love's embrace, we learn to fly.

Through gentle whispers, souls arise,
In the warmth of truth, our spirits prize.
In moments shared, our hearts align,
In every glance, the divine does shine.

In laughter's glow, we lose our fears,
With every heartbeat, joy appears.
Together wandering, hand in hand,
In sacred moments, we understand.

With nature's song, we dance through grace,
In each other's eyes, we find our place.
As star-kissed journeys come and go,
In love eternal, our spirits grow.

With every dawn, hope's ember glows,
In your embrace, my heart now knows.
In loving you, a world we create,
Elysium awaits, it's never too late.

Righteous Roads Converged

Two paths entwined beneath the sky,
In purpose grand, both you and I.
With each step taken, faith unfolds,
In righteous roads, our truth holds.

Together we stand, facing the dawn,
In love's embrace, we carry on.
Through mountains high and valleys low,
In unity's strength, our spirits glow.

In every storm, we find our way,
Through trials faced, we learn to stay.
With hearts steadfast, we choose to rise,
For in our bond, the promise lies.

In sacred trust, our visions blend,
In life's great tapestry, no end.
Together we walk, forever bound,
On righteous paths, where love is found.

With every step, our souls align,
In faith and hope, our hearts combine.
Two roads as one, we journey forth,
In love eternal, we find our worth.

Fortunes of the Bond Renewed.

In the stillness of the night, we pray,
Hearts entwined in faith, come what may.
Through trials faced, our spirits soar,
In love's embrace, we are evermore.

With every tear that graces the ground,
New beginnings in silence are found.
The ties we forge, divinely spun,
A testament bright, two lives as one.

When shadows drift, and doubts may rise,
We turn our gaze towards the skies.
With whispered hopes, and steadfast might,
Together we walk, into the light.

In sacred bonds, we find our worth,
A promise made at our sacred birth.
With open hearts, we trust and share,
In every breath, love's gentle care.

As seasons change, and time unfolds,
Our journey writes a tale retold.
In every blessing, grace resounds,
Fortunes shine in love that abounds.

Fleeting Grace

In morning's light, the world awakes,
Fleeting moments, the heart it breaks.
A whisper soft, from heaven's door,
Grace cascades, forevermore.

Each day a gift, wrapped tight with cheer,
Yet shadows dance, reminding us here.
With open arms, we greet the day,
In grace we thrive, come what may.

Through trials faced, we find our song,
In fleeting grace, we learn to be strong.
Embracing love, both wild and free,
We are the truth of divinity.

In breaths we take, in hearts that yearn,
Fleeting moments, we discern.
And when we fall, we rise once more,
For in His love, we are restored.

So let us dance in grace's flow,
With every heartbeat, love will grow.
In fleeting hours, together we find,
A glimpse of heaven, in heart and mind.

Echoes of the Heart

In silence deep, the heart does speak,
Echoes of love, both soft and meek.
Whispers of hope, entwined in grace,
A melody time cannot erase.

In every trial, the spirit shines,
Strength emerges, through sacred signs.
With each heartbeat, we sing our song,
In echoes of faith, we all belong.

Through valleys low, and mountains high,
With faith as wings, we learn to fly.
United in love, through the stormy weather,
We find our way, together forever.

In the rhythm of life, we find our place,
As echoes of the heart embrace grace.
In cherished moments, remember the art,
The boundless love that sets us apart.

Though time may fade, and shadows fall,
The echoes of love will always call.
In every dream, our souls will dance,
In echoes of the heart, we find our chance.

The Divine Reunion

In the quiet hush, where spirits meet,
A divine reunion, tender and sweet.
With open arms, we lift our gaze,
To the One who guides our days.

In every soul, a piece of light,
Illuminating the darkest night.
When we gather, hearts filled strong,
Together we sing the sacred song.

Every moment shared, a precious thread,
Weaving us closer, where angels tread.
With hands held high, we rise in grace,
In the divine reunion, we find our place.

Through trials faced and joys embraced,
Our spirits dance in love's warm grace.
In laughter and tears, we learn to see,
The beauty woven in unity.

So let us recall this sacred bond,
In every dawn, our hearts respond.
For in this reunion, pure and true,
We are forever, born anew.

The Celestial Dance of Affection

In the embrace of twilight's glow,
Angels weave a tapestry of light.
Stars hum softly, hearts in tow,
Love's melody takes flight.

With each step, the heavens sigh,
In rhythmic harmony, they sway.
To the sacred song that won't die,
Affection blooms in night's ballet.

Beneath the moon's watchful gaze,
Souls intertwine in pure delight.
A dance that spans the endless days,
Guided by the spirit's light.

When sorrow shadows the fervent soul,
This dance ignites the spark anew.
In unity, we are made whole,
An eternal bond, steadfast and true.

So let us twirl through time and space,
With faith as our celestial guide.
In every heartbeat, divine grace,
In love, forever we abide.

Resurrection of the Tender Spirit

Awake, dear heart, from slumber's chain,
The dawn calls forth a vibrant song.
From ashes rise, shed every pain,
In love's embrace, we all belong.

Like petals springing from the earth,
Our spirits bloom with colors bright.
In faith, we find our sacred worth,
Eclipsing darkness with the light.

A gentle whisper fills the air,
"Rejoice!" it sings to weary souls.
Together, we cast aside despair,
As hope within our being rolls.

Through trial's fire, we emerge fair,
Transformed by grace, forever free.
The tender spirit laid bare,
In unity, we find our plea.

So rise, dear friends, and hold on tight,
To love that resurrects and heals.
In every heart, a flame ignites,
A truth that neither time conceals.

Covenant of Longing Hearts

In silence dwell two beating hearts,
An unspoken bond, a sacred tie.
With each whisper, a promise starts,
In yearning gazes, love's reply.

Through trials faced and shadows cast,
They stand united, never torn.
A covenant forged, steadfast,
In every night, love's quietly sworn.

Though distance stretches, tides may change,
Their spirits soar with fervent grace.
In dreams, a world rearranged,
Where longing finds its rightful place.

Together they weave time and space,
In prayer, their hearts entwined anew.
Hope shines bright, a guiding trace,
In every heartbeat, love rings true.

So let this promise echo loud,
In the chambers of the soul's delight.
With every tear, love stands proud,
In a covenant that takes flight.

Sanctity in Reunion

In twilight's hush, two souls converge,
A sacred meeting, time holds still.
With gentle sighs, their spirits urge,
In love's embrace, they drink their fill.

Each heartbeat sings a hymn of grace,
As memories dance like autumn leaves.
In reunion's light, they find their place,
Within the web that love weaves.

Sacred whispers fill the night,
Promises made beneath the stars.
In every glance, the world feels right,
United, they carry love's scars.

For every longing leads to grace,
Through trials borne, they understand.
In every smile, the truth they trace,
Fate united, hand in hand.

So let the heavens break in cheer,
As hearts remember the sacred ties.
In the reunion, love draws near,
A journey crowned beneath the skies.

The Seraphic Touch of Memory

In the quiet of the soul's embrace,
Whispers of love in sacred space.
Angelic beams of light descend,
Through the veil, where sorrows mend.

Time weaves tales of grace divine,
In every heartbeat, a sacred sign.
Visions of joy in twilight's glow,
The seraphs sing of loved ones' flow.

Each memory a treasured prayer,
Echoing softly, beyond compare.
The heart is warmed by their soft touch,
In moments cherished, we feel so much.

Through trials faced, and dreams set free,
The seraphs guide us, through destiny.
With wings of peace, they lift us high,
In unity, we soar the sky.

In this dance of light and shade,
Every prayer a serenade.
The seraphic touch, oh, how it gleams,
A reminder of love that never seems.

Revelations in the Garden of Reunion

In the garden where spirits bloom,
Hearts converge, dispelling gloom.
Petals whisper of sacred peace,
In every breath, our souls release.

Beneath the branches, shadows play,
Revelations dawn with light of day.
Voices mingle in the breeze,
Love's embrace, the heart's true ease.

Here, the past and future meet,
In every moment, grace is sweet.
The ties of kinship gently bind,
Reunion's joy, a treasure mined.

Songs of old, in harmony,
Echo through this sacred tree.
Within these roots, our stories grow,
In faith and love, we come to know.

Each blossomed thought, a prayer in sound,
In the garden, peace is found.
Revelations sweet, forever laid,
In the light of love, we are remade.

The Echo of Cherished Voices

In the stillness, whispers weave,
The echoes of those who believe.
Time may fade, but love remains,
A symphony in joyful strains.

Each cherished voice, a guiding star,
Reminds us of how loved we are.
In the silence, we hear the song,
In every heart, where we belong.

They speak in dreams, in tender sighs,
A presence felt, beneath the skies.
Their laughter dances in the air,
In every moment, they are there.

Through valleys deep and mountains high,
Their echoes bloom, they never die.
A testament of love so pure,
In every heartbeat, we endure.

The cherished voices softly call,
In faith, we rise though we may fall.
Their whispers guide our weary way,
In love's embrace, we find the day.

Nectar of the Revisited Heart

In the garden of the soul's sweet quest,
Lies the nectar, a sacred test.
From seeds of hope, new blossoms spring,
In every heart, love's offerings.

The revisited paths we tread,
In memory's arms, our fears are shed.
With every sip, the spirit wakes,
In tender moments, the heart aches.

The nectar flows from wells divine,
Uniting us in heart and mind.
Each drop a promise, pure and bright,
A guiding star in the darkest night.

Through trials faced, we find our way,
In sacred love, we choose to stay.
With gratitude, we lift the cup,
In every heartbeat, we rise up.

So let us taste this love today,
In unity, we find our sway.
The nectar sweet, forever shared,
In the revisited heart, we dared.

The Light Upon the Forgotten Path

In shadows deep where silence reigns,
The guiding light breaks through the chains.
With whispers soft like morning dew,
It calls the heart of those who rue.

Through tangled woods where lost souls tread,
A beacon shines where hope has fled.
It illuminates each weary step,
And leads the lost to promises kept.

With gentle grace, it softly shows,
The way to joy where prayer still grows.
From broken dreams and burdens past,
It lifts the heart and holds it fast.

In every heart that seeks to find,
A touch of grace, a peace of mind.
The light abides in tender care,
Awakening love from deepest despair.

Oh path unseen where shadows creep,
With faith, I wander, faith I keep.
For in the night, the dawn will break,
And lead me home, my soul to wake.

A Harvest of Lost Promises

In fields where hopes lay barren, dry,
The whispers of past dreams still sigh.
Each seed of faith once boldly sown,
Now lies beneath the weight of stone.

Yet from the dark, new life will spring,
The dawn reveals what joy can bring.
In silent prayers, the heart's refrain,
Awakens strength from deepening pain.

O'er mountains high and valleys low,
The angel's wings begin to glow.
A harvest waits with open hands,
To gather hopes like golden sands.

The winds shall blow the dust away,
And in that light, my spirit's stay.
For every promise that was lost,
A journey awaits, no matter the cost.

In faith, I trust the seeds I've sown,
Through trials faced, I've brightly grown.
A tapestry of grace displayed,
In every tear, a light conveyed.

The Prayer of Returning Flames

Beneath the ashes, hidden bright,
The embers glow, a whispered light.
With hearts aflame, we lift our voice,
In prayer, we find our sacred choice.

As candles flicker in the gloom,
We beckon forth the fire's bloom.
Each spark ignites our weary souls,
Restoring hope, making us whole.

In unity, we bend the knee,
To seek the light eternally.
A prayer that stirs the stillness there,
Turning our hearts to grateful prayer.

O flames of love, rise high and strong,
In harmony, we sing our song.
With gentle hands, we share the glow,
A warmth that only truth can know.

And as the night gives way to dawn,
The prayer of flames shall carry on.
For every heart resolved in peace,
Shall find within, a sweet release.

Miracles in the Quiet Shadows

In quiet corners, softly framed,
The whispered love is still proclaimed.
Unseen, it dances on the breeze,
A gentle touch that seeks to please.

Oh, every heart that stops to pray,
Discovers hope in some small way.
Miracles hid from worldly sight,
Shining brightly in darkest night.

With every breath, a sacred trust,
In every glance, a grain of dust.
Yet from the earth, a flower grows,
A gift of faith the spirit knows.

In every sorrow, there's a grace,
Transforms the weary in this space.
For in the quiet shadows cast,
A miracle unfolds steadfast.

Embrace the still, the unseen hand,
That guides us gently, firm yet grand.
For in the heart, where shadows play,
The light of love shall find its way.

Celestial Threads Woven Anew

In heavens bright, our spirits rise,
Threads of love weave through the skies.
Guided by the divine embrace,
Mending hearts in sacred space.

Stars reflect our hidden dreams,
Unity found in gentle beams.
A tapestry of hope unfurls,
Binding souls in sacred swirls.

Each moment shared, a sacred thread,
In harmony, our hearts are fed.
Through trials faced, we learn to see,
The strength of love's pure tapestry.

In shadows cast, a light appears,
Whispers of grace dissolve our fears.
Hand in hand, we seek the light,
Through love's embrace, we find our sight.

Celestial songs, our voices raised,
In faith we stand, forever praised.
Woven anew, our spirits soar,
Together we'll forever adore.

The Rebirth of Kindred Spirits

In quiet woods, where shadows play,
Kindred spirits find their way.
Through whispered prayers and gentle sighs,
New life blooms beneath the skies.

Awakening hearts from weary sleep,
Promises made, our faith we keep.
In unity, we rise and strive,
Through love's embrace, we come alive.

Rebirth thrives where love takes root,
Nurturing seeds of hope, our fruit.
Beneath the stars, our dreams ignite,
With every dawn, we seek the light.

Giving thanks with each heartbeat,
In joyous dance, our souls we meet.
A circle formed of radiant grace,
Together in this sacred space.

Let kindness bloom, a fragrant flower,
In every heart, a boundless power.
With open arms, we share our song,
In harmony, where we belong.

Epiphany Beneath the Stars

In night's embrace, the stars align,
A sacred moment, truth divine.
Whispers flutter on the breeze,
Epiphany brings hearts to ease.

Each twinkling light, a guiding flame,
Calling forth our sacred names.
With open hearts, we stand in awe,
Revealing love's eternal law.

Dancing shadows, light entwined,
In silence deep, connection find.
The universe, a mirror clear,
Reflects the love we hold so dear.

Beneath the vast and endless sky,
Our spirits soar, we learn to fly.
In every pulse of cosmic time,
Together sing in sacred rhyme.

The stars shall fade, but love remains,
In every heart, its voice sustains.
Epiphanies like rivers flow,
In love's embrace, forever grow.

The Altar of Regained Devotion

At dawn's first light, we gather near,
An altar built to hold our fear.
With trembling hands, we offer prayer,
In devotion's fire, we lay it bare.

Through trials faced and wounds laid bare,
We rise anew, a bond we share.
In every tear, a lesson learned,
For in our hearts, true love has burned.

Regained devotion, strong and pure,
In sacred silence, hearts endure.
With every breath, a pledge we make,
To honor love, for love's own sake.

In moments shared, our spirits thrive,
Held close by faith, we feel alive.
In unity, our voices blend,
For every beginning bears no end.

Let gratitude like rivers flow,
In humble prayer, our hearts bestow.
At the altar, we unite as one,
In love's embrace, we've just begun.

Destined Embrace

In silence deep, a whisper flows,
Hearts entwined where the spirit knows.
With open arms, the heavens meet,
In love's embrace, our souls complete.

Beneath the stars, a calling high,
Guided by grace, we learn to fly.
In faith, we find our path so clear,
A destined touch that draws us near.

Moments shared, a sacred dance,
In every trial, a second chance.
Through joy and pain, the light remains,
In unity, love's essence reigns.

From shadows cast, we rise anew,
In every heart, a spark shines through.
With spirit strong, we walk our way,
Together bound, come what may.

With every breath, a promise made,
In faith we stand, unafraid.
Through storms we weather, still we rise,
In destined love, we find the skies.

A Reverent Promise

Beneath the veil of morning light,
A promise whispered, pure and bright.
In every tear, a sacred vow,
To hold the faith, to live the now.

In moments soft, where shadows wan,
The heart awakens, carrying on.
With hands extended, we shall mend,
Each broken soul, a cherished friend.

Through trials faced, we find our voice,
In steadfast love, we make a choice.
To rise with grace, our spirits soar,
In reverent trust, we seek for more.

With every dawn, a chance to start,
To live with grace, each gifted part.
In prayers we share, our hopes take flight,
In unity, we find the light.

Together bound, we find our way,
In faith, our hearts forever stay.
A promise kept through time and space,
In love's embrace, we find our place.

The Return of Light's Caress

When shadows fall, hope's song will play,
A gentle guide to light our way.
In the stillness, whispers call,
Embracing souls, we rise and fall.

Through darkest nights, we seek the stars,
In every wound, the healing scars.
The dawn will break, its golden hues,
In warmth's embrace, we'll find our muse.

As petals open, grace unfolds,
A tapestry of love retold.
In sacred space, our hearts align,
In prayerful breath, we intertwine.

Through faith renewed, we stand as one,
Embracing paths where hope begun.
In struggle fierce, we learn to see,
The light that lives eternally.

With every heartbeat, love's refrain,
In joy and sorrow, we remain.
The return of light's caress we seek,
In unity, our spirits speak.

In the Garden of Forgiveness

In quiet blooms, the heart does mend,
In soft whispers, we extend a hand.
Among the thorns, a beauty grows,
In the garden where compassion flows.

Each tear that falls, a seed is sown,
In sacred soil, love's truth is grown.
With every breath, we rise anew,
In the warmth of grace, our spirits glue.

Through trials faced, we learn to see,
In every soul, the spark of glee.
Forgiveness thrives where love abides,
In open hearts, the pain subsides.

In gentle hands, we craft the way,
With hope unyielding, come what may.
In every bond, we find our peace,
In the garden, our hearts release.

With petals soft, we touch the sky,
In love's embrace, we learn to fly.
In forgiveness found, we claim our might,
In the garden's glow, we find the light.

The Beacon of Beloveds

In the stillness of the night,
A light shines, pure and bright.
Guiding souls through shadow's veil,
Whispers of love's sacred tale.

With every step upon this path,
Hearts entwined, we find the math.
Unity in spirit's grace,
In each other's warm embrace.

Echoes of the prayers we send,
A circle strong that will not bend.
Through trials, joy, and all we face,
The beacon shines, a holy space.

In moments lost, we search for more,
The love we seek, a golden shore.
In togetherness, we are made whole,
The beacon lights the way for soul.

Let us lift our voices high,
In harmony, we reach the sky.
The beloved's flame, a sacred trust,
In love's embrace, we rise from dust.

Hymns of the Rejoined

From distant shores, we come anew,
Hearts reborn, in skies so blue.
A melody of love resounds,
In each heartbeat, grace abounds.

With every note, our spirits soar,
Echoes of peace forevermore.
Together in this sacred dance,
We are the light, we take the chance.

Voices raised, a chorus wide,
Unified by love, our guide.
In this hymn, we find our song,
Together, where we all belong.

Through valleys deep, we journey long,
In faith and hope, we grow more strong.
With each refrain, we intertwine,
In the embrace of the divine.

Let the heavens hear our praise,
In every heart, a sacred blaze.
Together, we shall walk in light,
Our hymn of love, eternally bright.

Rituals of Heartfelt Reunion

In the sacred space we gather near,
Fingers intertwined, love sincere.
With open hearts, we greet the dawn,
In unity, our worries are gone.

Rituals weave a tapestry,
Of lives reborn, now wild and free.
Each moment shared, a precious gift,
As spirits soar, we rise and lift.

The fragrance of hope fills the air,
In every word, a silent prayer.
Exchanging glances, souls connect,
In togetherness, we find respect.

Time may part us, yet we remain,
In the echo of joy, there's no pain.
The warmth of love shall always bind,
In these rituals, our hearts aligned.

With grace we honor, with faith we stay,
For in togetherness, we find our way.
The reunion glows, a gentle spark,
Illuminating paths through the dark.

Miracles of the Spirit's Touch

In quiet moments, blessings flow,
A gentle breeze, our spirits know.
The touch of grace, so soft and near,
Transforming sorrow into cheer.

Miracles unfold in silent nights,
As stars above illuminate our sights.
In every heartbeat, we find our trust,
In the spirit's flow, we feel the just.

Through trials faced, we gather strength,
In unity, we go the length.
Each little miracle, a sign,
Of love divine, ever entwined.

With open hearts, we seek and find,
Through every doubt, we stay aligned.
The spirit's touch brings peace anew,
A bond unbroken, tried and true.

In every laugh, in every tear,
The miracles remind us to draw near.
With faith as our guide, we shall embrace,
The spirit's whisper, our sacred place.

Reflections of a Timeless Bond

In the stillness of the night,
Whispers of love take flight.
Heaven's grace shines like a star,
Guiding souls from near and far.

Through trials we find our way,
In faith's embrace, we softly pray.
Bound by a promise divine,
In unity, our hearts align.

Each moment a precious light,
Illuminating shadows of night.
With every tear and every smile,
We walk together, mile by mile.

In silence, solace we find,
In love's mirror, two become one mind.
An eternal dance, a sacred art,
A reflection of the beating heart.

Let the world fade away,
As we bask in love's pure ray.
For in this bond, we are whole,
A timeless tale, the deep soul's scroll.

The Celestial Reawakening

Awake, O spirit, arise anew,
In morning's light, a vivid hue.
Nature's hymn, a sigh through trees,
Reminds our hearts of sacred pleas.

The stars descend in gentle grace,
Illuminating every face.
With each breath, the cosmos sings,
Of endless love and holy things.

In the stillness, hear the call,
The whispers breeze through all.
Let your worries drift like steam,
Awakening hope, a tender dream.

Mountains high, oceans wide,
In creation's arms, we confide.
From ashes rise, let spirits soar,
For love is the ever-open door.

Every dawn unveils the truth,
Renewed in joy, as in youth.
Together we tread this sacred path,
In the heart of love, we find our math.

Prayer for the Heart's Homecoming

O gentle guide, hear my plea,
Lead my heart back home to Thee.
Within Your arms, I find my rest,
In the quiet, I've been blessed.

With every heartbeat, I seek light,
In shadows deep, I crave Your sight.
Restore my soul, renew my grace,
In love's embrace, I find my place.

Let each prayer like petals fall,
Lifting gently, answering the call.
In the stillness, let me hear,
Every whisper, every tear.

Guide my journey through the storm,
In faith's embrace, I am reborn.
With humble heart and open mind,
In Your presence, peace I find.

O sacred light, shine bright and clear,
Drawing near, dispelling fear.
In every moment, lead me home,
In love's vast cradle, I will roam.

The Wandering Heart's Rejoice

Wanderer, come and heed the call,
In the gentle breeze, find it all.
For every step is a sacred quest,
To seek the love that knows no rest.

Through valleys low and mountains high,
Let your spirit learn to fly.
In the dance of life, embrace the chance,
To find your peace in love's sweet dance.

In every stranger's smile, behold,
A story woven, a love untold.
With open heart, we walk as one,
In every setting sun, a new begun.

For in the journey lies the grace,
Embracing all in God's warm embrace.
Turn your gaze to the sky above,
For every beat whispers of love.

Rejoice, dear heart, for the road is wide,
With faith as your guide, in love abide.
The wandering soul will find its way,
In joy and peace, come what may.

Milton Keynes UK
Ingram Content Group UK Ltd.
UKHW031320271124
451618UK00007B/190